My name   _____

My phone #   _____

My violin teacher   _____

I0459082

Lines & Spaces

FOR VIOLIN

BOOK 1

Note-Reading Companion
to Kaleidoscopes for Violin

BY ELISE WINTERS

KALEIDOSCOPES

Lines & Spaces, Book 1: Note-Reading Companion to Kaleidoscopes for Violin, Second Edition

© 2025 Kaleidoscopes for Violin, Austin, Texas. All rights reserved.

ISBN 978-1-959675-13-6

First Published 2016. Second Edition 2025.

Copyright © Elise Winters, 2016, 2025

Lines & Spaces, Book 1: Note-Reading Companion to
Kaleidoscopes for Violin, Second Edition, by Elise Winters

© 2025 Kaleidoscopes for Violin, Austin, Texas. All rights reserved.

ISBN 978-1-959675-13-6

Copying of individual pages for personal use is permitted. Any other copying, digital transmission,
or digital storage of this book in whole or in part is prohibited without written permission
obtained beforehand from the publisher.

TABLE OF CONTENTS

NOTE-READING

WRITING & CHORDS

TEACHER NOTE

Lines & Spaces is designed as a companion to the *Kaleidoscopes for Violin* series. Its prequel, *The Musical Looking Glass*, Book 1, builds a foundation of understanding for students' musical literacy through moveable-do solfege, basic piano fluency, guided discovery, and creative play.

The reading exercises and folk songs in *Lines & Spaces* can be used as a note-reading companion to any other method book or repertoire series.

If the teacher wishes to additionally use the chord decoding and song notation exercises scattered throughout the book, we suggest referencing the corresponding songs in the *Kaleidoscopes* repertoire recording. Alternatively, the teacher may find equivalent recordings of these beloved folk songs to help acquaint their students with them.

All of the *Kaleidoscopes* albums are available to stream on Spotify, Apple Music, and other major platforms. Links to these recordings, as well as further information about *Kaleidoscopes*, can be found at discoverviolin.org.

THE KALEIDOSCOPES RHYTHM SYSTEM*

Duple Meter		
Quarter note	♩	TA
8th notes	♫	TA TE
16th notes	♬♬	ta ka te ka
32nd notes	♬♬ ♬♬	ta ma ka ma te ma ka ma
Triple Meter		
Quarter note	♩	TA
8th notes	♫♩	TA TU TI

* adapted from the syllables developed by Edwin Gordon, the originator of Music Learning Theory

Draw the Treble Clef

We use the DO clef 𝄠 so that we can sing a melody starting on any note we want to. All that matters is that the melody has the right sound and rhythms. We use the solfège names of the notes: *do, re, mi*, etc.

Usually, though, composers like to tell us EXACTLY what notes to play, so that when two people play together all of the notes match.

When we see a treble clef 𝄞, we know that each line or space belongs to a specific *pitch*. We call these pitches A, B, C, etc. The "swirl" part of the clef wraps around the note "G." For this reason it is also called the "G clef."

Learn to draw treble clef signs following the steps below. Complete one staff of practice drawings each day.

Reading D, E and F♯

For each line of music:

1. Read (speak) the note names.
   Note: The name of F♯ in English is "F sharp," but is much easier to say the German name, fis ("fees"), in rhythm.

2. Play the line on the violin.

D = open D string
E = first finger on D
F♯ ("F sharp") = second finger on D

Adding G and A

For each line of music:

1. Say the names of the notes out loud.
2. Keep the beat by tapping on your shoulder. Now speak the rhythm using rhythm language.
3. Say the note names out loud, in the correct rhythm.
3. Play the melody on the violin.

D E F♯ G A

G = third finger on D
A = 4th finger on D (or open A string)

5.

6.

7.

8.

9.

10.

11.

Write the D String Notes

Write the notes indicated using quarter notes.

- Notice that the note heads are elliptical and slightly tilted, rather than circular.
- Make sure to place any sharp in *front* of the note it pertains to.

Do one set of notes each day this week until you finish the page.

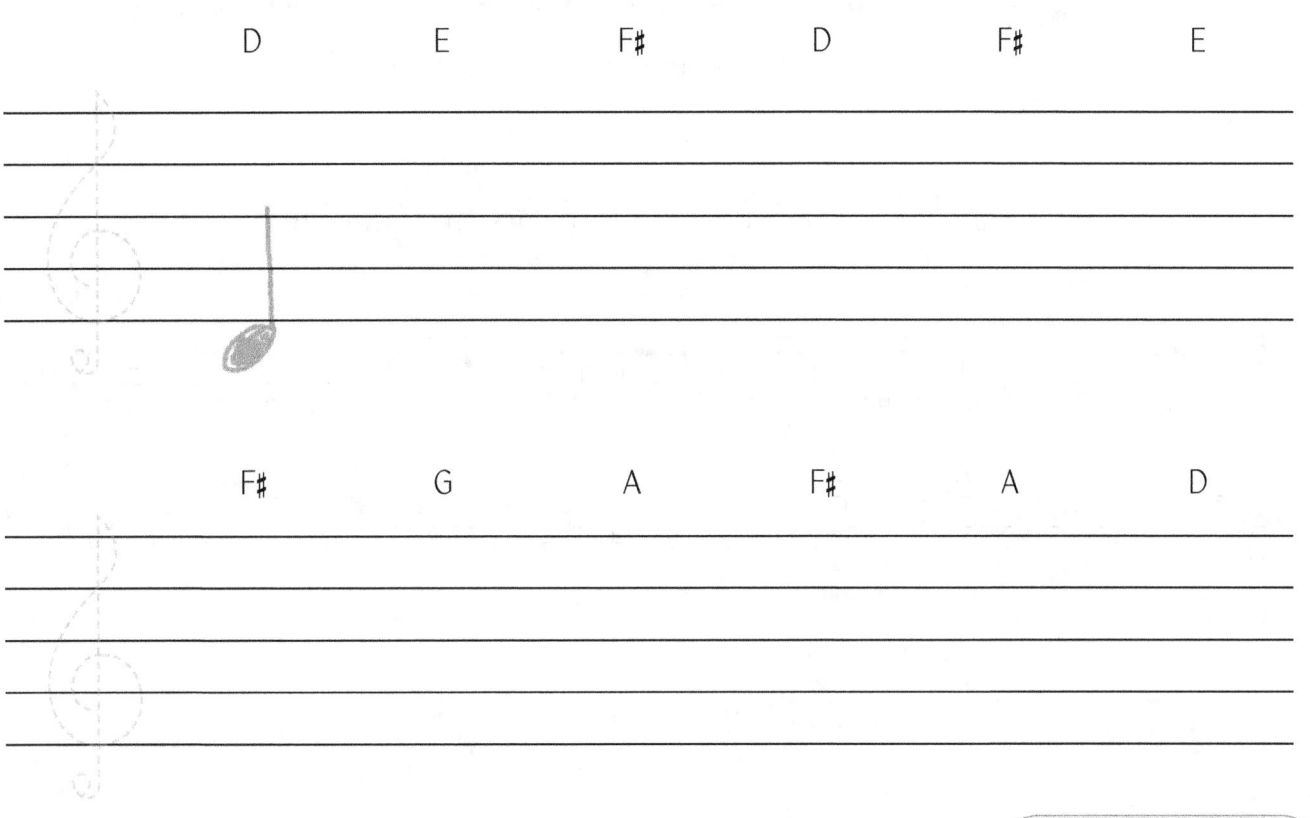

D   E   F♯   D   F♯   E

F♯   G   A   F♯   A   D

Let Us Chase the Squirrel

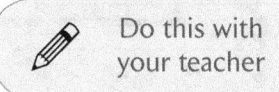
Do this with your teacher

Play "Let Us Chase the Squirrel" starting on open D string.

Now write the notes and rhythms for the *first four beats* of this song, played on this string.

You will have ♩ and ♫ notes. Be sure to use a F♯!

For each line of music, 1) Say the names of the notes out loud; 2) Speak the note names in the correct rhythm (with faster and slower notes), tapping the beat on your shoulder. Finally, 3) Play the melody on the violin.

Túrót Ettem

"TOO-rote ET-tem" · I Ate Cottage Cheese

Hungarian

"I ate cottage cheese, dropped it, I don't even know where I put it."

一番星みつけた・Ichiban Boshi Mitsuketa

ichi-BAN BO-shi mits-kay-TA
I Found the First Star

Japanese

Als Ich Einmal Reiste

When I Was a Young Lad

German

Hoffnung Giebt Trost

Hope Gives Comfort

German

Moj Chlopek

"moy CHLO-pek" · My Lover

Polish

Chords on the piano

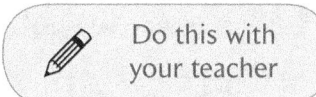

1. Play two notes on the piano that are a step apart. Try this in many places on the piano.
2. Now play notes on the piano that are skips apart. Try this in many places.

When we play notes at the same time on the piano, they sound good if they are skips apart. This is called *harmony*.
Two skips stacked together are called a *chord*.

When we play violin in a concert, we have a pianist who plays notes that *harmonize* with our solo.

Every chord has three notes (demonstrate), but at the beginning we can play just the *bottom two* notes.

Chords to "Hot Cross Buns"

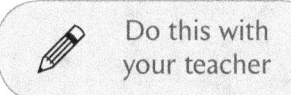

1. Play "Hot Cross Buns" on the piano, with the right hand, making sure one finger is on every key.
2. Now, in a lower octave, play the notes DO and MI at the same time. This is the DO chord.
3. Play the DO chord on the beat while the teacher plays the melody of Hot Cross Buns.
4. Are the any places where the DO chord clashes with the melody notes? Play the song slowly to listen.
5. Our other favorite chord is SO chord. Practice jumping between DO and SO chords.
6. Now your teacher will play Hot Cross Buns again. Try playing the SO chord any place where DO chord sounds clashy.
7. When you have chosen the chords you like, write them in the boxes below. D = do chord, S = so chord.

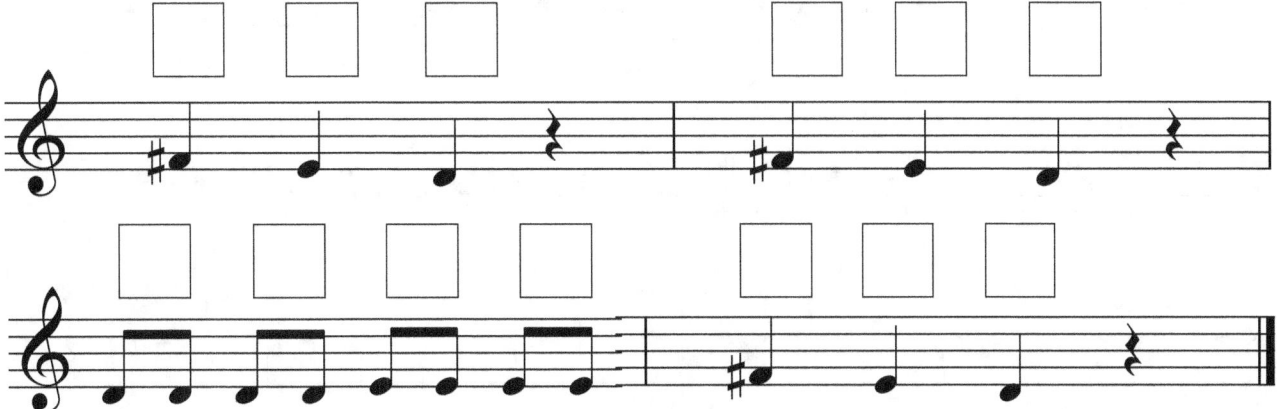

Hot Cross Buns: Two Hands

1. Practice jumping between DO chord and SO chord.
2. Play the chords while your parent plays the melody.
3. Then play the melody while your parent plays the chords.
4. Finally, practice playing Hot Cross Buns with left-hand chords and right-hand melody (at the same time). Have fun!

Reading B, C#, D & E

For each line of music:

1. Say the names of the pitches out loud. For C# ("C sharp") use its German name, *cis* ("sees").
2. Speak the pitches in the correct rhythm, tapping the beat on your shoulder.
3. Play the melody on the violin.

A   B   C#   D   E

B, C#, D = 1st, 2nd and 3rd fingers on A string
E = open E string, or 4th finger on A string

13.

14.

15.

16.

17.

Schönster Schatz

Beautiful Treasure

German

かえるのうた・Kaeru no Uta

ka-e-ru no u-TA
The Song of the Frog

Japanese

Obkročák

An Obkročák ("ōb-cro-chak") is a traditional Czech stepping dance.

Czech

ほたるこい・Hotaru Koi

"HO-ta-ru koi"
Come, Firefly

Japanese

Write the A String Notes

Write the notes indicated using quarter notes.

- If the note is below the middle line, its stem is placed on the right, pointing UP. ♩
- If the note is above the middle line, its stem is placed on the left, pointing DOWN. ♩
- If the note is on the middle line, its stem can go either way.
- Here is a helpful way to remember which side the stem goes on: Your notes should look like p's and d's (puppies and dogs) rather than 6's and 9's.

	A	B	C♯	D	E	A

	B	D	B	A	D	B

All My Little Ducklings

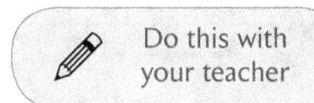

Do this with your teacher

Play "All My Little Ducklings" starting on open A string.

Now write the notes and rhythms for the *first four beats* of this song, as played on the A string.

You will have ♩ and ♫ notes. Be sure to use a C♯!

Quarters on D and A

Moving Eighths on D & A

27.

28.

29.

30.

31.

Write the Sharps

The German song below, "Borsorge," is in D major. Write in the missing sharp (♯) each place the note F appears. Then play the song.

Сабадашко Моя · Sabadashko Moya

My Sabadashko

Ukrainian

Note: Sabadashko is a Ukrainian family name.

Levántete, Juana

Get Up, Juana

Spanish

Esta Muchachita

This Young Woman

Spanish

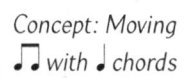

Concept: Moving ♫ with ♩ chords

Chords for "Mary Had a Little Lamb"

1. The teacher or parent plays "Mary Had a Little Lamb" on the piano, while the student plays a two-note DO chord on each beat.
2. Where does the DO chord not fit? Find where to play the SO chord.
3. Practice together until the chord changes are familiar.

   At home: Play the melody of "Mary Had a Little Lamb" with the right hand, while playing the chords in the left.
   Add the sharp sign wherever F♯ appears below.

Papagaio Loiro

Blonde Parrot

Portuguese

In this children's song, a young woman asks the golden-beaked parrot to deliver a letter to her boyfriend.

Tres Cautivas

Three Captives

Spanish

La Muñeca

"la mu-NYE-ca," The Doll

Spanish

J'ai d'un Bon Tabac

I Have Some Good Tobacco

French

Fine

Da Capo al Fine

Pomme de Reinette

"PUM duh reh-NET" • Pippin Apple

French

Roulez Chemins de Fer

"ROO-lay SHEH-mah de fehr" • Ride the Railroads

French

Teacher

虫のこえ・Mushino No Koë

mu-SEE-no ko-EH • Cricket Song

Japanese

Minha Saia Nova

"MEEN-ya SAH-yah NO-va" • My New Skirt

Portuguese

Teacher

Notes on the E String

When speaking the pitches in rhythm, G# ("G sharp") use the German name, *gis* ("jees").

E F# G# A B

Write the E String Notes

Write the notes indicated using quarter notes. Since the notes are above the center line, their stems will point *downward*.

E   F#   G#   A   B   E

Do this with your teacher

Let Us Chase the Squirrel

Play "Let Us Chase the Squirrel" starting on open E string.

Now write the notes to the SECOND phrase of this song—i.e. the last 8 beats— as played on the E string.

You will have ♩ and ♫ notes. Be sure to use a G#!

Eighths on E

39.

40.

41.

42.

43.

Phoebe in Her Petticoat

English

Quand J'Etais Petite

"cohn zhe-TAY pe-TEET" · When I Was Little

French

Beau Temps d'Automne

"boo tah da-TEM" · Beautiful Autumn Days

French

Fine

Da Capo al Fine

Write the Sharps

In A major there is one sharped note on the A string, C♯. There are two sharps on the E string, F♯ and G♯.

1. Write the note names below.
2. Add the sharps appropriate to A major. Put stems on all the notes.
3. Then play the notes to check your work.

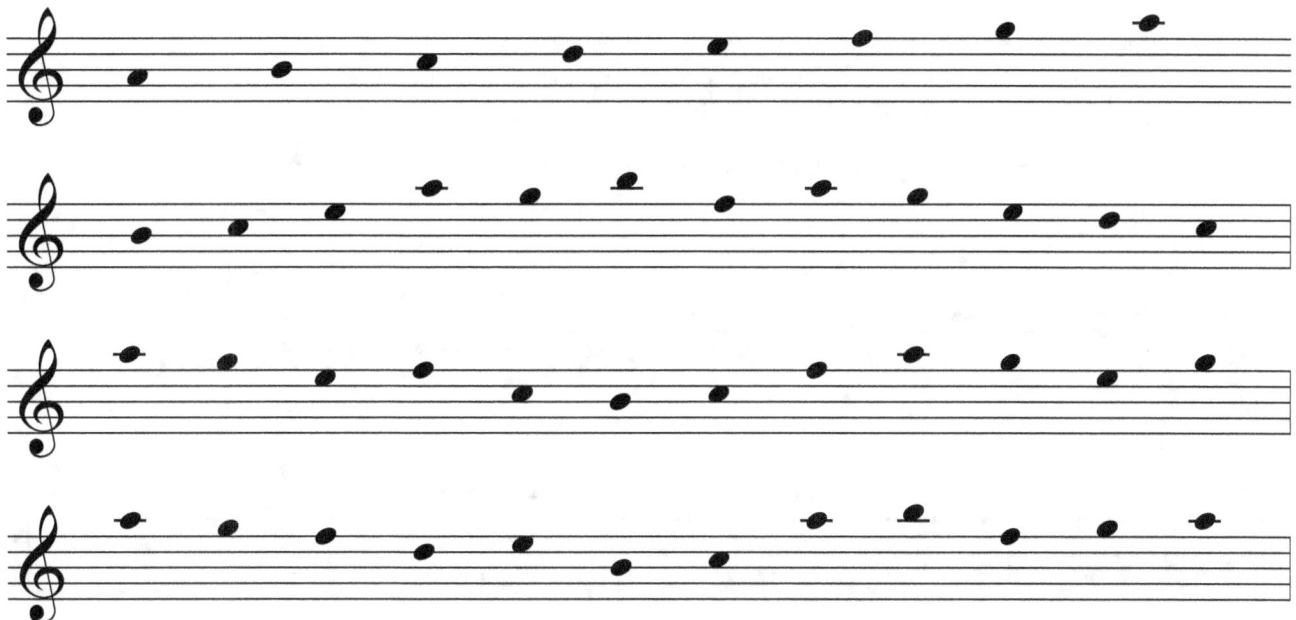

Bateau, Ciseau, La Rivière, La Rivière

"BAA-to, SEE-so, la reev-yair, la reev-yair"
Boat, Chisel, River, River

French

Notice the sharps written at the far left of each line. This tells us to use all the sharps that belong to E major. This is called a *key signature*.

Teacher

This is slightly nonsensical children's song about a river which overflows its banks into the town streets.

Chords to "Ducklings"

Concept: FA chord

1. The teacher plays "All My Little Ducklings" on the piano while the student plays a two-note DO chord on each beat.
2. Where does the DO chord not fit? Find where to play the SO chord.
3. Are the any places where the SO chord also does not fit? What other chord might work instead?
4. Practice together until the chord changes are familiar.

Home practice: Play "All My Little Ducklings" with melody and chords together.

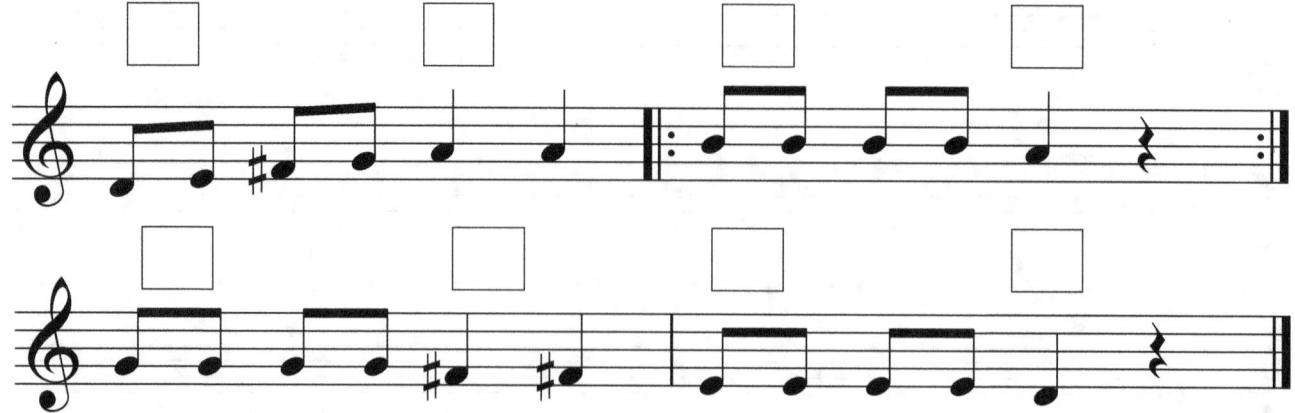

24

Slurs on D, A and E

Reading in G Major (with added C♯)

Qui Marierons-Nous

"kee mar-YEH-roh noo" • Who Will Marry Us

French

うさぎ・Usagi

"Uh-SAH-gi," Rabbit

Japanese

Два Голуби Пили Воду • Dva Golubi Pili Vodu

Two Doves Drinking Water

Russian

Chords to "Boil Them Cabbage"

Figure out the chords to the song below. Play the song with melody and chords together, and practice until it is fluent.

One chord has been suggested for you (the FA chord below DO). What chord might also work in this place? Which one sounds better to you?

Note: When a sharped note happens more than once in a measure, only the first one needs the sharp.

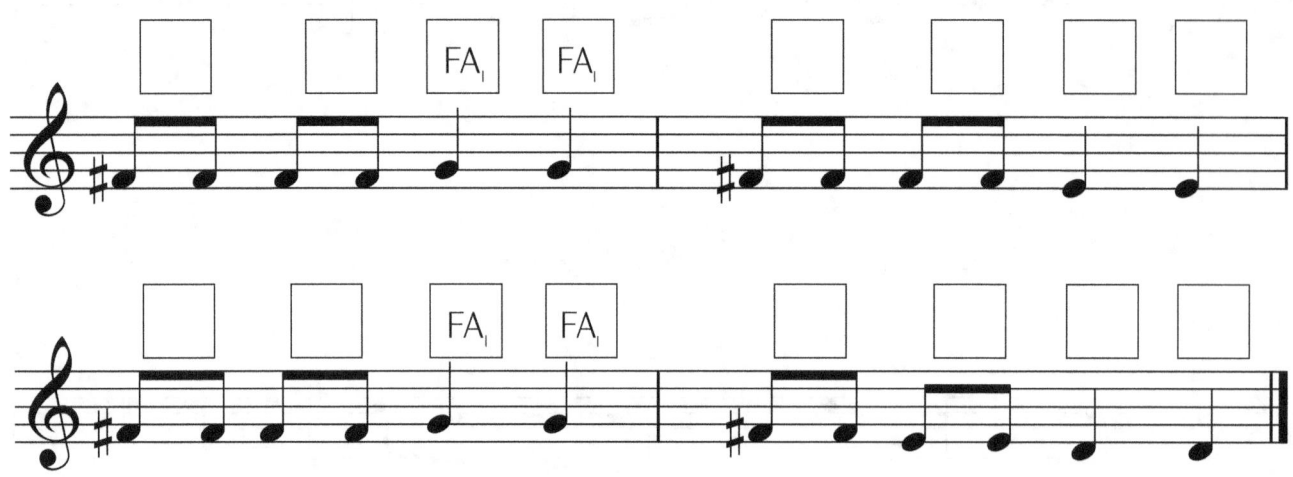

でたでた　つきが ・ Deta, Deta, Tsuki Ga

"DAY-ta, DAY-ta, tski-GAH" • The Moon Came Out

Japanese

28

数え唄 · Kazoē Uta

"ka-ZO-ee oo-TAH" • Counting Song

Japanese

L'Ane et le Loup

"LEN ih leh LOO"
The Donkey and the Wolf

Croatian

Rezniček

"REZ-nee-CHEK" · The Butcher

Bohemian

Notes on the G String

A, B, C = 1st, 2nd and 3rd fingers on G string
D = open D string, or 4th finger on G string

The key signature tells us that each printed F—regardless of octave—should be played F♯ unless marked otherwise. Summarizing the usual sharps in this way makes any exceptions (added sharps, flats, or naturals) more obvious. The composer may offer a reminder in parentheses (♯) when helpful.

56.

57.

58.

59.

60.

61.

Write the G String Notes

Write the notes indicated using HALF notes.

```
        C       B       A       G       B       A
_____
_____
_____
_____
_____
```

```
        D       G       B       A       D       A
_____
_____
_____
_____
_____
```

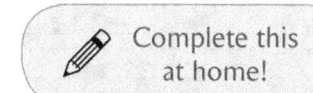
Complete this at home!

All My Little Ducklings

Play "All My Little Ducklings" starting on open G string.

Now write the notes and rhythms for the *first four beats* of this song, played on this string.

You will have ♩ and ♫ notes.

```
_____
_____
_____
_____
_____
```

Ой На Горі Дубина · Oy Na Gori Dubina

On Mount Dubina

Ukrainian

En Revenant d'Angoulême

"ah RUH-vuh-NAH dah-gou-LEM"
Returning to Angouleme

French

Dubrovnik Kolo

The kolo is a traditional Slavic circle dance, known as the "horo"
in Bulgaria and "oro" in Macedonia. Dubrovnik is a city in Croatia.

Croatian

小马快快走 · Koma Kai So

"KO-ma ky so" · Pony Running Fast

Japanese

Колись Моя Стара Ненька · Kolis Moya Stara Nienka

"KO-lees MO-ya, sta-RA ny-en-KA"
Once Upon a Time My Old Mama

Ukrainian

Unglück und Glück

Unhappy and Happy

German

Certificate of Completion

Awarded to

_____
Name of violinist

for completion of

Lines & Spaces Book 1

On this _____ day of _____
      Date   Month, Year

_____
Teacher signature

www.ingramcontent.com/pod-product-compliance
Lightning Source LLC
Chambersburg PA
CBHW081543120626
46550CB00009B/2849